TaNisha Fordham

THE EGOT

Circa 1989

Books by TaNisha Fordham:
"Go Black Boy Fly"
Pop! Pop! A body drops. What happens next? Well... That's the plot.

Films by TaNisha Fordham:
"Queen"
A feature documentary about minority women in pageantry.

"Go Black Boy Fly"
A narrative feature about 5 black brothers on an epic bicycle adventure.

For more information visit our website:
www.enlightenedvisions.org

A special note...

In 2020, in the wake of the murders of Brianna Taylor and George Floyd, I wrote, *12 Mo' Angry Men,* a raw and unabashed narrative about black voices and communities: how we are impacted by violence against us and how we might think about justice in the face of so many injustices. *12 Mo' Angry Men,* a reimagined take of *12 Angry Men,* by Reginald Rose, explores the themes of justice, blackness, community, black culture, and how we show up for one another... *and sometimes don't.*

I never would have imagined 1 short year later *that* production would have the opportunity to do a short (3 day) run off-off Broadway (at the LaTea Theatre) at the same time I was making my Broadway Associate Directorial debut on the musical *Company.* There's been something very serendipitous about it all. Reginald Rose's son Jonathan came to see *12 Mo' Angry Men* on our closing night and emailed me some thoughts following the show; his short, yet impactful, words are still flying around in my head in this moment; "Be safe and take courage."

It isn't lost on me how often I have to take courage here at the Bernard B. Jacobs Theater. Even as one of the associate directors on the team I often feel out of place; it's no one's fault, really. No one is *"doing"* anything, specifically. I don't have war stories, necessarily, about some great injustice that's been directed at me. In fact, I was first selected as a directing fellow/apprentice with the Black Theater Coalition (BTC) for the rehearsal process of *Company.* But then, the producer and director of the production decided to keep me for the run of the show; they saw me. They acknowledged me and validated that I was contributing in this space. Yet still, I feel most days like I've felt most of my life:

I just don't quite fit.

At this juncture I have decided that it isn't the titles/positions/accolades that I'm waiting on for validation. I mean, I've done nothing at all and yet by God's grace I've done so much. I've co-produced a film that was Oscar nominated, I've served as Mrs. NJ United States, I've placed top 11 at the Mrs. United States Pageant, and was voted "Mrs. Congeniality" and "The People's Choice" in both of these systems (respectively)... *And there's more.* I've directed over 30 original productions spanning several mediums, I've published a book (this book will make two), I've produced the first ever theater in the park event for the largest city in the state of N.J., I've been selected as a resident with programs at Columbia University, Rutgers University, and a coalition on Broadway… *And, there's more.*

But that's the point --- the more doesn't mean anything. There will always be someone more accomplished and all the accomplishments in the world don't give us any more value than someone who's sole accomplishment is being alive.

This piece is an ode to that.
This piece is an ode to those who are wholly alive.

I'm thankful, each day, for every opportunity, and accolade, and title, and experience that God has granted. But, this piece is my thank you to God for the things that are most important of which maybe no one will ever acknowledge the importance:

I'm thankful for my grandparents who have already headed home to glory but loved me with such a specific love that I still feel their arms wrapped around me today. They paid for my college tuition so that I could just dream --- out loud --- and write silly plays and go to school for a major that so many people have been told is silly, silly, silly. I get to live this *silly life,* on Broadway, because my grandparents believed in me when I was stacking pillows on the floor and wrapping a towel on my head and singing full voice, "Part of Your World," from *The Little Mermaid.*

I'm thankful for my mom who had me at 19 but proved to me, even then, that I didn't have to let others define me. Mom could've been the stereotype --- single, teen mom, lost in a big world. **No!** Mom graduated college in 3 years-and-change. Mom got 2 master's degrees. Mom works in one of the most affluent communities in Western N.Y. as an English teacher: the only black teacher in her school. Mom is a super(s)hero in every way.

I'm thankful for my husband --- my best friend in the world. My monkey… He is the best friend that I could've ever asked for. We're literally twin souls. He's a man of God, he's quirky, handsome, smart (has a PhD), and he's the sweetest man in the entire world; he's literally never met someone who doesn't immediately fall in love with him - it's impossible not to do so.

I'm thankful for my dog who sat in the stroller for hours and hours as I walked 10+ miles daily in the 100+ degree Arizona heat because I was trying to walk my way out of debilitating anxiety. My little Scoop Treat would always stare from the back of the stroller with his big wide open eyes, "It's ok mommy --- you aren't alone --- even in hellish heat, I'm with you. And, we'll get through this together."

I'm thankful for God… *Just God…* **For everything…** <u>An endless list</u>. For reasons that I will never be able to put in words.

Aren't those things award worthy?

And, we all have those things in our lives. And, that doesn't even scratch the surface. It would take a play unto itself to list all the things in my life that are impeccable in this way. And, I am hopeful that this gives you an opportunity to take inventory on your life, too.

The final note: this is my story… *Sure.* It's based on events that have happened in my life and people that I've known personally, ***but this is our story.*** This is your story. And, I hope that you will not wait any longer for approval or a title or validation.

I hope, my friend, that you will decide today that you are enough because you are. **<u>You are.</u>** And if life is hemming you up, trying to make you feel otherwise… Don't negotiate with life ---

SNATCH YO' FREE.
It belongs to you…

Dedicated to <u>you</u>…

*Now, what <u>**you**</u> gone do?*

Mrs. United States Pageant weekend; 2019

EGOT
/ˈēgät/

noun INFORMAL | US

The achievement of having won all four of the major American entertainment awards (an Emmy [television], a Grammy [music], an Oscar [film/motion picture], and a Tony [live Broadway theater]).

IN THAT ORDER

THE EGOT
A Thought (Chapter 1)

Broadway Associate Director Debut (Company Musical); December 9, 2021.

THE EGOT
A Thought (Chapter 1)

I ain't waiting to be counted.

Ha!

For **_you_** to pick me?
I'm not waiting to get free.
It be what it be.

This girl: *this <u>one</u> here* ---
you gon' get what you see.
I ain't got nothin' else, think we all can agree:

We' just wasting our time sittin' 'round to be tapped.

We waitin' for this.
Then we waitin' for that.
What we waitin' for, bruh?
The time is now.
'Nother second of waiting, I can not allow…

Ain't nobody gone choose you.
<u>You ain't gone be tapped.</u>
Our world simply isn't….

It ain't set up for that.

Even as I type: the red squiggles… *and blues-*
Are correcting my words
Tryna lay down the rules.

The world ain't for rebels.
What… ***you got a cause?***

I hope you ain't waitin' or 'spectin' applause.
The world is set up for herding the sheeple.
I ain't no sheeple though...***people.***

So much is wasting:
Time...
Thought...
And the waitin', I reckon', it's mostly for naught.

I'm finally peepin' the secret, the key:

<u>I ain't waitin' on nothin' *'cept me.*</u>

I don't need no approval to pick up my pen.
I don't need no one else, I can simply begin.

The praise and the blame...
They just 'bout the same
But, the name of the game
Is stop chasing the fame.

Stop chasing the fame,
That's the name of the game.
'Cause the blame got you crazed
And the praise is to blame.

It ain't about fame.
If you're blamed,
If you're praised
Keep this in frame:
Play ***<u>your</u>*** best game.

So this one right here ---
This goes out to the homies;
The world may not give you a treasure or trophy.

The world may not get---
You're ahead of your time...
And, too far ahead is treated as crime.
But, way out ahead is paving the way.
And, way out ahead, despite what they say;
Is what change the world.

That is a fact.

I'm leaving that there:
Ain't no rhyme beat for that.

This jawn here
This one's for the fam:
My mama.
My hubby.
And both of my grands.

For Jesus the Christ:
The Lord above Lords.
I done told y'all already --- *not mincing these words.*
For Buffalo, Newark, for Greensboro, too.

And nah, I ain't done.
But, what *you* gone do?

I'm creating this moment
So now ---
I'm. Is. Free.

I'm the E. I'm the G. I'm the O. I'm the T.
I'm done waitin' for someone to give it to me.

I'm takin' what's mine.
I'm snatchin' my free.

I'm not bound by the rules.
And... NO I AIN'T DONE.

.

.

.

Yo!
This joint right here's 'bout to be fun.

Yea, this one right here,
This is for you.
The world needs... *yea, it needs... **yea, it's needing you, too.***
You can be what you want ---

Sure, an E.G.O.T.

Or, wait:
better yet ---
What you lookin' like free?

Some'uh'ya'll folks **I done already lost.**
This piece here is spicy: <u>you' gettin' this sauce.</u>

Emmy or Grammy Or Oscar or Not...
I'm thinking and writing and saying my thoughts.
Tony or Oscar or Grammy or bust.
I'm seeing the value in all of my stuff.

Because, who decides?
You?
Is it... You?

The worth of ***<u>my life</u>*** is determined *by who?*

The worth of my life --- is determined by me --- and I'm thinking I'm worth all the
E. G. O. T.s

I Ain't Waitin' On You
A Song for Self (Chapter 2)

Somewhere in Newark, N.J.; circa 2019.

I Ain't Waitin' On You

A Song for Self [Chapter 2]

I Ain't Waitin' On You
I Ain't Waitin' On You

Ou--Ou--***OUUUUUU!***

I Ain't Waitin' On You
I Ain't Waitin' On You

No More -- uh -- ou -- OUUUU!

I Ain't Waitin' On You
I Ain't Waitin' On You

I Ain't Waitin' On You
I Ain't Waitin' On You

Child, who?
On you?
Oh no.
NO MORE.

I Ain't Waitin' On You
I Ain't Waitin' On You

Ou--Ou--***OUUUUUU!***

I Ain't Waitin' On You
I Ain't Waitin' On You

No More -- uh -- ou -- OUUUU!

I Ain't Waitin' On You
I Ain't Waitin' On You

I Ain't Waitin' On You
I Ain't Waitin' On You

Child, who?
On you?
Oh no.
NO MORE.
No sir.
Not me.
Ouu we.
Child please.
Can't be.
Bayyybeee.

I Ain't Waitin' On You--
Ha! Waiting on who?

I Ain't Waitin' On You--
Ha-Ha-Ha **<u>this fool!</u>**

I Ain't Waitin' On You
I Ain't Waitin' On You

I Ain't Waitin' On You
I Ain't Waitin' On You

Child, who?
On you?

Oh no.
NO MORE.

No sir.
Not me.

Ouu we.
Child please.

<u>Can't be.</u>
Bayyybeee.

Girl bye.
You lie.

I ain't waiting on you no more.

__In the Beginning__
A Poem (Chapter 3)

Front porch fun; circa 1990.

In the Beginning
A Poem (Chapter 3)

Yo:
At the top,
No, Not at the end:
Where else did you think we were gonna begin?

Way… Way back…
Back before time…
Back before blackness was treated as crime…

Back before racism ---
Sexism, too.
Way before me…
Talkin' way before you;

Back in the day…
Before we were young---
Before the sun,
Before time had begun…

Way.
Way.
Way.
Way.
Way.
Way.

Waaaaaaaaaaaaaaaay.

Way.
Way.
Way.

Ok... Ok...

Way
Way
Way
Way
Way
WAY-BACK.

I was foreknown.
<u>The setting was black:</u>

Blackness: *empty.*
Blackness: **dark.**
Black, like soil.
Black at the start.
In the beginning, yo: black ***ran*** free.
Black like, black like, black like... me.

A deafening silence.
And nothing around.
A deafening silence.
A dizzying sound.
A deafening silence.
No woman. No man.
Desolate, vacancy filling the span.

Not even a soul.
An empty space:
Not town,
Nor village,
Not even a place.

But in that abyss:
I was foreknown.
But, only by God and God alone.

God:

> ***"She!***
> We'll make another she.
> We'll make... We'll make another she.
>
> She gone... she gone... she gone be:
> Boundless. Bounding, bountifully.
> She gone fly. She gone beeeeeee...
>
> Ou. This girl ---
> She gone be free.
>
> She'll have eyes.
> This girl will seeeeeeeeeeeeeeeeee.
> She got...She got...
> Destiny.
>
> She got... She got... She got.
> Glee
> And spring and sprite and sprite and spree.
>
> Glee?
> *Yea.*
> She?
> *Yea.*
>
> She gone be:
> Bursting. Brimming.
> She gone be:
>
> > > *She!*
>
> We'll make another she.
> She gone... She gone... She gone...

Beeeeeee.

She got… She got… She got…
Me.

So:
She. Is. Gone. Be. Free."

I was foreknown.
The setting was black:
But that was:
Way,
Way,
Way,
Way-Back.

I was known. Known ***before***.
God called me out.
But wait. There's more;

Way.
Way.
Way.
Way.
Way.
Way.

Waaaaaaaaaaaaaaaay.

Way.
Way.
Way.

Ok… Ok…

Way.
Way.

Way.
Way back in the day.
Way back; I was fore-ordained.

GOD:

"Go.
This girl will go, go, go.
Low. Then high. Then high. Then low.

Whether high or on the flo',
Where we lead
I know she'll go.

Send her.
Send her far and wide.
To the call she will abide.
Casting down the ache of pride.
Casting down the will inside.

Go.
She'll go.
She'll go, go, go.
Toe to heel then heel to toe:
Toe-heel-heel.
Heel-toe.
Heel-toe.
Heel-toe-heel.
Then toe some mo'.

Even when she's feelin' low.
She'll look up,
Then up some mo'."

Fore-ordained.
And yes.

Fore-known.

Me and God.
Us, all alone.

God almighty--
God alone.
Sitting on that great big throne,
Sitting in His great big home:

> Knew me.
> *Knows me.*
> **I am known.**

I've been destined ---
So it's said.
And, I knows it -- in my head.
But:
Sometimes, when I look out,
All I feel is fear and doubt.

This black skin.
That's what they see:

They:

> "She a... She a... She a...
> *SHE.*
> She ain't... ***Nil***...
> How could ***she*** be?

> She ain't nothin'.
> *Ain't a he.*
> **And.** She black.
> She ain't ---

> *Right!*

She ain't… She ain't… She ain't…
White.

She ain't quiet.
She too loud.

Brave…
Too bold…
Too tall…
Too proud…

She gone… She gone… She gone…
Be…
Think she setting captives free?"

This black skin ---
And this hair…
And this body…
Dare… How dare…

And my she-ness.
And my God.
None of it do ***they*** applaud.

And my strength,
Cause I ain't weak.
And, my stutter.
And, my speak.

I got… I got… I got…

Ay…
I got me.
What can I say?

Known…
Predestined…
Way, way back…
Back when everything was black.

Lately, though, I've been appalled.
Lift my head:
To God I call.

Lift my head and tilt it back.
Screaming with a strain and crack:

"God.
Oh God.
<u>What shall I do?</u>

God:
Oh God,
Please.
Please, come through.

What, oh what…
What shall I do?
World is aching.
Only you…

Only you can see us through.
Sickness.
Suff'rin'.
Dyin', too.

You gone… You gone… You gone…
You…?
God, we need you to come through.

Where you at, God?
Where you be?
Oh, dear God of destiny…

Where you at, God?
Where you ---
Oh…"

Everything around me slowed...

"I can see y'all --- *in the crowd.* And, the angels --- *in a cloud.* I can see y'all *all around.* Look at us; we is profound… We gone… We gone… We gone be… All together **we gets free.** Me and you and you and me… You got… I got… We got: *we.*

What you… *What is you gone do?* Help me see this vision through? I got you… And, you got me… We got… We got… We got… We. We got… We got… Gots-the-key.

We ain't waiting for our free.

We got… We got…
Gots-the-key.

We. Is. Gone. Be. Free."

Oh my Lord --- a booming sing
Sounding like a freedom ring…

God:
    "GO!"

Me:
    "What's that?"

God:

 "GO! I say."

Hear His voice so clear, today.

God:

 "GO! I say.
 And, don't look back.

 Get the white and brown and black.
 Get the sick
 And, get the poor.
 Get them. And then get some more.

 Go. Go. Go.
 You. Yes you.
 You is asking what to do:
 You called me,
 I'm calling you.

 You gone… You gone… You gone…
 Oooooou:

 You gone be my heart, my hand.
 You gone go, *then go again.*

 You feel sad?
 You feel appalled?
 Good.
 'Cause you've been called."

Way.
Way.
Way.

Way.
Way.
Way.

Waaaaaaaaaaaaaaaay.

Way.
Way.
Way.

         Ok... Ok...

Way.
Way.
Way.
Way.
Way.
Way-back.

We were known, ***ordained... in fact.***

We are called,
Bein' justified:
Couldn't change it if we tried.

We can help impact this story
Looking towards expected glory.

Lift-
Lift-
Lift-
Lift-
Lift your hands.

Lift them up.

Then, up again.

Lift your hands up.
Lift them high.
Lift your hands up towards the sky.

Open hands,
Now open hearts…
Get this jawn here from the start…

We gone… We gone… We gone… Be…
"We" is you… is us… is me…

We got… We got… Destiny.

We. Is. Gone. Be. Free.

Your hands!
Your hands!

It's in your hands.

Keep them up.
And, up again.
In your hands and in your heart.
That's where freedom start.

Put them down?
Nah!
Lift 'em up.

Up… Said up…. *Said up…* **Said up!**

We… is you… is us… is me…
TOGETHER WE IS FREE.

Little Girl [BLACK]
A Memoir in Rhyme (Chapter 4)

Mom & Me, Tonawanda N.Y.; circa 1990.

Little Girl [BLACK]
A Memoir in Rhyme (Chapter 4)

A.
B.
C.
D.
E.
F.
G.

I was a little ole girl as sweet as tea.

H.
I.
J.
K.
L.
M.
N.

World shot me down, *then shot again.*

O.
P.
Q-R...
Q-R...
S.
Would I do it again?
Said yes. ***Said yes!***

T.
U.
V.
W.
X.

Don't be anxious. Don't be stressed.

Y.

You want to know why?
<u>Please.</u>
We all gotta learn them ABCs.

I was a little ole girl.
Pure at heart.
Had drama for yo' mama right from the start.

I was a little ole girl.
6 or so.
In a green t-shirt wit'a matching bow.

I was a little ole girl
In an all white school.
Brown girls live by different rules.

I was a sweet little girl,
As sweet as tea.
Had friends as far as the eyes could see:

Jamie. Sarah. Lauren. Jen.
These little ole girls were my best friends.

Hannah. Margaret. Taylor. Jan.
We played each day then played again.

Ally. Holly. Desi. Anne.
And, of course, the other Jan --
One was blonde, and one brunette;
The best friends that a girl could get.

Alyssa. Bridget. Carly. Sue.
Black girls?
Um. *Well, maybe 2.*
Me and *yes* my "sister…" *Friend*;
The two black girls: ***they called us twins.***

But, *mostly just a sea of white:*
Ask me: I fit in alright!
Ask me: I felt right at home.
Never did I feel alone.

In a sea of blondes and blues
I'll tell it once,
I'll tell it true:
Black and nappy, askin' me,
Had its place
And, I was… free.

In a sea of blondes and blues
I was free in blissful bloom.
Pollyanna: ***unprepared.***
Pollyanna: ***not a care.***
"Pollynisha" *in an all white schoo'…*
But, what's a little -*brown*- girl to do?

What's a little -*brown*- girl to do?
What's a little -*brown*- girl to do?

Skinny waists,
And bone-straight hair:
Brown girls entered
If we dared.

"Barbie" songs sung in the hall.

On top of it all,
I had the nerve to be tall.

But, I was home as home could be:
Sweet little girl,
As sweet as tea.

I was home as home could be:

Ignorant *but* free.

What a sweet, little, girl I was back then:
Calling everybody "friend."
Thinking all the folks was kin,
Even kin with different skin.

I was happy.
I was green.
Didn't have a drop of mean.
Hadn't seen what I hadn't seen.
Until this playground scene:

Girl:

"Your hair."

Me:

"*Thanks.*
I get it from my mama.
Get it from my mama.
Get it from my mama."

Girl:

"She did it?"

Me:

"Yep!

In my pajamas.
In my pajamas.
In my pajamas."

Girl:

"What is it?"

Me:

"Braids."

She was staring like a llama...
Staring like a llama...
Staring like a llama...

Girl:

"Oh-"

Sigh...

I knew there was a comma.
I knew there was a comma.
I knew there was a comma.

Girl:

"Oh. I just ask 'cause..."

Here go' the drama.
Here go' the drama.
Here go' the drama.

Girl:

"Your hair looks--"

Oh man...
Here comes the trauma.

Here comes the trauma.
Here comes the trauma.

.

.

.

.

.

Jamie. Sarah. Lauren. Jen...
Were supposed to be my best, good friends.

Hannah. Margaret. Taylor. Jan...
Stared me down then stared again.

Ally. Holly. Desi. Anne...
And, of course, the other Jan;
One Jan stared and one Jan spoke,
Centering me inside this joke.

Alyssa. Bridget. Carly. Sue.
Black girls?
What were we gon' do?
Me and *yea* my *"sister..."* "friend;"
The two black girls: *they called us twins.*
But now, in this big laugh barrage
Twin was trying to camouflage.
Twin won't tryin' to be the joke.
Twin kept staring with the other folk.

Ask me --- I was feeling lost.
Wisdom has a lofty cost.
Never had I felt alone.
I *thought* I was right at home.

From a sea of blondes and blues,
I tell it now;

I tell it true.

Staring eyes forgot their tact:
We see you as *__black.__*

Girl:

"Your hair."

Me:

"Thanks.
…I get it from my mama.
Get it from… my mama.
Get it… from my mama."

Girl:

"She did it?"

Me:

"Yea?
…In my pajamas.
In… my pajamas.
In my pajamas."

Girl:

"What is it?"

Me:

"…Braids?"

Then she stared like a llama.
Stared like a… llama.
Stared like a… llama.

Girl:

"…Oh."

Ugh!

I knew there was a comma.
I knew there was a comma.
I knew there was a comma.

Girl:
> "…Oh, I just ask 'cause…"

Here go' the drama…
Here go' the drama…
Here go' the drama…

Girl:
> "Your hair looks--"

Oh man…

Here comes the trauma --
Here comes the trauma --
Here comes the trauma --

Girl:
> *"Your hair looks **weird.**"*

… … … … … … … … … … … … … … … … .
… … … … … … … … … … … … … … …
… … … … … … … … … … … … … …
… … … … … … … … … … … …
… … … … … … … … … …
… … … … … … … … … ..
… … … … … … … ..
… … … … … …

… … … … …
… … … …
… … … .
… …
…
.

In a sea of blondes and blues…
I **was** free in blissful bloom.
Pollyanna, ***unprepared.***
Pollyanna, ***not a care.***

Pollynisha: *In an all white schoo'…*

And, what's a little --sweet-- brown girl to do?
What's a little --sweet-- brown girl to do?
What's a little --sweet-- brown girl to do?

Weird.
Commandeered.
And, I heard it so clear ---
These friends I revered,
Had sudd'ly appeared.
No one mocked.
No one jeered.
Though my faith had been smeared.
Weird. *I was weird.* **_I was weird._**

I can not say that much has changed.
Least not what is in my brain.
Silly as I'm sure I'll sound ---
And I know it ain't profound…

But, I still love Jan and Jan.
Hannah. Margaret. Taylor. Anne.

Ally. Holly. Desi, too.
Alyssa. Bridget. Carly. Sue.

That's what Pollyannas do:
Keep my "me" alive and true.

But…
What I know
I know for fact;
World see me, they seein' black.

<u>Change</u>
Random Musings (Chapter 5)

Posing in the front yard; circa 1990.

Change
Random Musings (Chapter 5)

We got skinny waists,
And bone straight hair!
Brown girls enter,
If you dare...
We're centering "other..." *As the joke.*
So, any of you "other" folk:
Race, religion, gender, skin,
Come on over,
<u>Enter in.</u>
You are family.
You are friend.
<u>*But; you still what you've been.*</u>

We got beauty standards,
Standards high!
Other folk,
You're free to try!
Other folk, try your hand
At reaching standards high and grand.
All are welcome!
Others, too.
All are welcome!
Come on through.
You are family.
You are kin.
<u>*But, you still what you've been.*</u>

Equity! *Inclusion, too!*
We got us; <u>we wantin' you!</u>
Diversity!
We want 'em all.
Midgets, mid-sized, super-tall.

Pasty white to chargrilled black.
Straight and queer;
We're doubling back.
We <u>LOVE</u> you, although *you're strange.*
Now…
All you have to do is… **<u>change.</u>**

<u>The Ogre on the Bus</u>
A Memoir in Rhyme (Chapter 6)

Summer camp fun in a skort and twists (second from the left); circa 1996.

The Ogre on the Bus
A Memoir in Rhyme (Chapter 6)

In middle school,
I was so cool.
Rode the bus on-down-to school.
Rode the bus.
Sat in the back:
Rosa Parks-somewhere-havin'a-heart-attack.

In middle school,
I rode the bus:
That yellow joint **I loved so much.**
I was gettin' older --
Talkin' 'bout **grade** 6
When bones didn't break from stones and sticks.

Mama was young:
29.
Well…
*27 for the **second time.***
Mama was young
And, I was too.
What two little brown girls s'posed to do?
10 years old,
And 29.
Sorry, 27… *for the second time.*

My first day of middle school:
I was shining like a jewel.

Hair in braids.
Brand new clothes.
Really, only Heaven knows
How one little girl could be so grand.

Mama was my biggest fan.

Lip gloss poppin'.
Teeth: real white.
New book bag: strapped on real tight.
Pencils. Binders. Folders. Pens.
Crayola crayons: *I had the brands.*

Pencil bag.
Hole puncher, too.
I was about to ***act-a-fool.***
Scissors. Notebooks.
Loose leaf paper.
Glue sticks, too. Oh!!! --- *and a stapler.*

I ***probably*** had a change of clothes.
Swear it:
Only Heaven knows how one little girl could
Ball so hard.
I was making it rain index cards.

I had markers and erasers.
Reinforcements for my papers.
Rulers. A protractor, boo.
My circles did what circles do.

I had a lunch box filled to brim:
A sandwich, chips, a soda and ---
Gummies! **LITTLE DEBBIE CAKES!**
Oh the hearts I was goin' to break.

And that ain't it.
No --- there was more:
Watercolor paints, galore.
Paints in every color known.

Mama was seated on a throne.
At 29 my mama knew ---
Knew what only mamas do;
Mama bought me all the stuff
The world would steal enough...

Walked on the bus.
Feelin' great.
I mean, **come on**, for Heaven's sake.
Walked on the bus.
Sat in the back.
My middle school plan was right on track.
Sat on the bus.
Sittin' in the rear.
Looked out the window:
Mama Dear.
Mama dear was waving bye.
Tellin' y'all: I was flyin' high.

I loved that bus.
Oh. ***Every bit.***
On that yellow bus I'd sit
With my friends I'd laugh; I'd play.
I didn't ride it every day.
Somedays, **sometimes**, mama drove.
But really only heaven knows the joy I had...
That yellow ride:
Made me feel alive.

Heading home,
One day,
Yes --- *on the bus;*

This story make' me wanna cuss.

One day a girl
All big and fat

Came hobblin' towards the bus's back.
Big-ole, juicy-ole, ugly, troll.
High school surely took its toll.

This big ole girl --- looked 42.
She couldn't've been in middle schoo'.
Came down the aisle with moistened breaths.
Stopped next to me -- breathing down my neck.

HuunnhhhnggG HhAaaaaaaaah
HuunnhhhnggG HhAaaaaaaaah
HuunnhhhnggG HhAaaaaaaaah
HuunnhhhnggG HhAaaaaaaaah

Big-ole, juicy-ole, ugly, troll…
Ugly, juicy, big and old.
Came, *I'm sure*, to ruin me.
Wasn't likin' what she see.

Ugly-ole, juicy-ole, big-ole troll...
Juicy, ugly, big and old.
Stankin', mean and big and rude…
Filthy, stankin' attitude.

She wasn't liking all my cool ---
Too -much- cool for middle school.
High school ogre mean and fat,
Wasn't down with that.

Stringy hair.
And, ugly face.
Sucking air out of the place.
All around I heard the chatter
Not the kind that flattered:

"What's her name?"

"I don't know."

"Don't really look like 6th grade, though."

"Don't really look like 8th grade."

"True."

"I hear she *ain't* in middle school."

"What's she doing on our bus?"

"Tired of gettin' teased and stuff."

"They transferred her."

"To ride with us?"

Intruder on the bus...

That day, that bus forever changed.
My yellow bus became estranged.

This ugly, stanking-ole, piece of poo,
Came, I'm sure, to stop my groove.

"MOVE!"

The ogre shouted move.

"Stare at me?
I'll stare at you.
Move, little girl.

Move.
Right now."

I couldn't even move my brows.
I couldn't even blink my eyes.
To my surprise, <u>I tell no lies:</u>
I was frozen, ***frozen stiff.***
Body parts would not submit.

Arms and legs they wouldn't lift ---
Not a movement, not a shift.

"Are you retarded?"

Whole bus stared.
She caught me unprepared.

"Please-Please-Please-Please-Please-Please-Please.
Please God, please…"

… With knocking knees ---

"Please-God-Please:
I'm begging you…"

I… mustered… up… *a scooch.*

That mean-ole-girl all full of slop.
Sat-on-down with a great big plop.
Sat down, yes, on top of me.
Against the bus, I had to squeeze.

That mean-ole, ugly-ole,

GROWN...

***...

CHILD...

Stole my ride --- my magic mile.
Stole my ride --- stole part of me.
Stole my joy... *my free.*

Doors close.
Engine on.
Seat. Belt. Clinks.
Windows squeak.
Children laugh.
My. Heart. Sinks.
Ogre burps.
Ogre shifts.
I shift, too.
What *is* a little brown girl to do?

Red light.
Green light.
Bus. Moves. Slow.
Friends play.
I sit:
All alone.
Ogre takes up space.
What could I do?
Least, thank God, the sky's still blue.

Bus stops.
Boy stands.
Reached--first--stop.
Boy leaves.
Doors close.
My heart drops.
My stop's soon.

My angst, it grew.
What was this little brown girl gone do?

Doors swing open.
Once, then twice.
We stop again.
Up to thrice.
One more stop.
And then it's me.
Sudd'nly I had to pee.

Reached my stop:

"Excuse me, please."

Ogre sat, ignoring me.

"Please!"

I say.

"Excuse me."

Nope.
Ogre takin' me as joke.

"Got to go."

Doors part.
Yelling now, and gaining heart:

"Please!"

I said...
A little louder...

Then of course,
I cowered.

Doors close.
Bus moves.
My. Heart. Race.
Ain't. A.
Move -- Ment.
In. The. Place.
Ogre stares.
Ogre shifts.
I shift, too.
Ma was about to act a fool...

"Where've you been?"

"I'm sorry mama.
Ogre caused me so much drama.
Ogre caused me so much trauma.
Hemmed up... *Caged:* just like a llama."

Mama put me in pajamas.
Mama, like the Dalai Lama
Rocked me.
Soothed me with a coo.
That's what mama always do.

And,
Ma was young:
29.
Well,
27 for the second time.

Ma had me at just 19.

But oh, such wisdom had she gleaned.

So… that next day --
The very next.
Mama sent me,
Spirit vexed,
Mama sent me on that bus,
Though I know it may sound rough,
Mama sent me on that bus
Said,

"Go take back yo' stuff!
Go.
Go back.
Go take yo' stuff.
Yo' stuff.
Go back.
Go' get yo' stuff.
That stuff?
That stuff…
Belongs to us.
Yo' stuff.
Yo' stuff.
It ain't enough.
A sorry?
No.
No, that won't do.
That stuff.
That stuff
Belongs to you.
Go.
I say.
Get on that bus.
Said,
Go take back yo' stuff!"

That next day of middle school
I was kind-of low.
Mama dropped me off that mornin'
Moving really slow…
Mama tell me somethin' though
That I didn't know:

> "Mama got you front to back;
> **God got you -- head to toe.**
>
> God got you inside--out, lil' girl.
> He got you all around.
> You haven't even got to call ---
> Least of all aloud.
>
> God little girl;
> God got you.
> Got you where you lack.
> And *mama* got you,
> little girl,
> Back to front to back."

In middle school,
Thought I was cool.
Rode the bus on-down-to school.
Rode the bus.
Sat in the back:
Not foreseeing an attack.

In middle school.
I rode the bus:
That yellow joint ***I loved so much.***

Until the ogre: big and mean
Came stomping on the scene.
That ugly-ole, juicy-ole, ogre -- mean:
She wasn't even green.

School ends.
Bell rings.
My. Heart. Aches.
Grab bags.
Run out.
Bus. Doors. Shake.
Tiptoe on.
Run to back.
Deep. Breaths. *Too.*
Dear God. Please.
Oh, Please;
Come through.

Sit down.
Stand up.
All. Looks. Clear.
Sit down.
Time ticks.
Feel-ing. Fear.
Engine cranks.
Engine runs.
My heart beats.
I. Feel. Fear. Down. To. My. Feets.

Time slowed.
Time slowed.
Time slowed down.
I looked.
I looked.
All around.

Ogre appears:
Then heads to back.
I could've had a heart attack.

"Move!"

She screamed.
The whole bus stared.

"God... "

I prayed, but I got scared.
Could not pray.
So,
I decided to move.
What else was a little brown girl gone do?

One stop.
Two stops.
Three stops.
Four.
Five.
Then six.
We stop some more.

"Dear God... *I...* "

I had no words.
This ogre bit was for the birds.

We passed my stop.
I didn't budge.
Don't you sit there being a judge.

Squeaky bus bounced down the road

With a heavy load.

Mama was young:
29.
Well…
*27 for the **second time.***
Mama was young
And, I was too.
And, two little girls got lots to prove.

Little babies:
Mom and me.
Bound to set the captives free.
Mama always came on through ---
*That's what **my** mama do.*

We were close to ogre land,
Bus was heading 'round the bend.
Raised my head.
Raised my chin.
Raised my eyes.
Raised them and:

Mama!
Standing on her throne.
She was standing all alone.
She was waiting on the route.
And, I let out a shout.

"You're in trouble.
I told my mama.
I told my mama.
I told my mama.

She's right there!

It's about to be some drama.
About to be some drama.
About to be some drama.

I'm a child of God.
Ain't no comma!
Ain't no comma!
Ain't no comma!

My mama.
My mama.
My mama.
My mama.

My mama!
My mama!
My mama!
My mama!"

She was only 29.
Just a baby.
So now, looking back, this story sounds crazy.

Ran off the bus to mama's arms.
That ogre girl was so alarmed.
Ma' set her straight.
"A talkin' to…"
'Cause that's what two little girls can do.

I faced my ogre.
Mom faced me.
Two little girls, we snatched our free!
Mom faced my ogre.
I faced mom.
Together: such a healing balm.

What is two little girls gone do?
Change the world,
Got lots to prove.
And, I suggest you clear the way.
'Cause we're **still** out here taking names.

<u>Back That Thang Up</u>
A Song for Mama (Chapter 7)

Mom in the mirror at the after party,
Company Musical Broadway Opening; December 9, 2021.

Back That Thang Up
A Song for Mama (Chapter 7)

I get it from my mama.
We gone back that thang up!
I get it from my mama.
We gone back that thang up!

I ain't e'en playin'.
We done switched the game up.
See what I'm sayin'?
We done switched the frame up.

Go best friend!
That's my best friend...
Go best friend!
That's my best friend...

Go best friend!
That's my best friend...
Go best friend!
That's my best friend...

This fo' my mama.
This fo' my mama.
This fo' my mama.
This fo' my mama.

Go Take Back Yo' Stuff
An Interlude (Chapter 8)

Go!
Go back.
Go get yo' stuff.

Yo' stuff.
Go back.
Go' get yo' stuff.

That *stuff?*
That stuff…
Belongs to us.

Yo' stuff…
Yo' stuff.
It ain't enough…
A sorry?

No!

No, that won't do.

That stuff.
That stuff
Belongs to you.

Go.
I say.
Go take it back.
Ain't no shame in that…

"They took it."
Fine.

Go snatch it 'gain.

<u>"They took it."</u>
Fine!

"They" cain't be friend.

"They" cain't be fam.
"They" cain't be kin.

They took it.
So!
I'm sorry…
And?

Who took yo' stuff?
Who took it?
Who..?
Who took yo' things?
Go get 'em foo'.

Go fool…
Don't just give it up.
We talkin' bout **YO'** stuff.

Taking Flight
A Short Poem (Chapter 9)

Mrs. NJ photoshoot; circa summer 2019.

Taking Flight
A Short Poem (Chapter 9)

The bird shuffled his feet.
Adjusted his legs.
He closed his eyes.
He lifted his head.
He tucked his wings.
Did not check on the weather.
He trusted the strength of his feathers.

The bird shook out his nape.
Straightened his crown.
Felt the wind blowing all around.
But, he opened his wings
And bent his knees.
With faith he took off to the breeze.

<u>**Running Girl Black**</u>
A Poem (Chapter 10)

*My grandma, Freddie Mae Fordham (the original "Running Girl Black"),
on her typewriter.*

Running Girl Black
A Poem (Chapter 10)

Running girl…
Running girl…
Running girl black…
Run girl…
Run.
Girl: *don't look back…*
Don't look back, girl…
Go on…
Run.
Run towards the…
Run towards the…
Run towards the sun…

I was born.
I was sunshine:
Bright like light.
Caramel wrapped skin.
Joy stuffed in tight.
I danced and I sang.
And, I'd run and I'd run.
I was running girl…
Running girl…
Running for fun…

Running past the wind.
Running through trees.
Bending…
And twisting…
And bopping my knees.
Running and dancing and kicking -- *with shout.*
I had to let the sunshine out.

I had to let the sunshine in:
Through breaks and cracks and ruptured skin.
My breaks my cracks were all from play ---
I was running all…
Running all…
Running all day…

Run to grandmama, first.
Run to grandpapa, next.
Run to mama.
Yes.
Ma knew my running the best.

With a running girl smile.
With a running girl cry.
I would open my arms
I would leap through the sky.

I was running girl….
Flying girl…
Couldn't stop me…
I was running way past where the eyes could see.

I was:
Running girl…
Running girl…
Running girl black…
I ran.
And, I ran.
And, *I'd dare not look back…*
I would ***dare not look back…***
I would run.
And, I'd run.
I would:
Run towards the…

Run towards the…
Run towards the sun…

I was levitating.
Lifting off *into life.*
I was fighting the wrongs.
I was making them right.
With a laugh and a smile and a leap and a spring.
I was running to…
Running towards *everything.*
I was running to…
Running *towards*…
Running **with** life…
Nothing was wrong…
All was right…

I was hugging and kissing and laughing with cheer.
I was running less…
Running less…
Less of fear…

I was running for nothing…
I didn't know why…
It would start in my toes…
Then spring into my thighs…
Then a bursting run would claim arms and then back.
I was having a…
Having a…
Running attack…

I would…
Run Forest…
Run Forest…
Run Forest…
Ruuuuuuuuuuuuun…

And, like Forest, my running had barely begun.

I was joy: *unabridged.*
I was happy: *unknown.*
I was soul: *content.*
And, *never alone.*

I was innocence: *honored.*
A sparkling glee.
Free.
I was free.
I was free.
I was free.

Freedom and running:
They somethin' the same.
Mr. Free and Ms. Run know each other by name.
You can't run 'til you're free.
May, with freedom, we run?
And my prayer's that our free days have finally begun.

Run girl.
Run girl.
Run girl black.
Never.
Said nah:
Don't you ever look back.
You can't run home, girl.
So --- run on.
Run as far as the day is long.

Yes.

Run girl.
Run girl.

Run girl black.
Run girl.
Keep your pace in tact.
Go girl.
Run girl.
Run girl.
Go.
Where you'll stop nobody knows.

I was teeth.
I was lips.
They were curved towards the light.
I was twirling, by day.
I was dancing, by night.
But I never stopped running.
Never, I swear.
I was running without a care.

Feet pounding the ground.
And my head lifted high.
I was wholly…
Yes wholly…
Yes; wholly *alive…*
Knees bending and stretching…
Arms swift at my side…
I couldn't've stopped if I tried.

I knew no bounds.
I was running girl black.
I've got to get that feeling back.
I knew no bounds.
I don't know why,
This story brings tears to my eyes.

Run girl.

Run girl.
Run girl black.
Never.
Said nah:
Don't you ever look back.
You can't run home, girl.
So --- run on.
Run as far as the day is long.

Yes.

Run girl…
Run girl…
Run girl black…
Run girl…
Run.
Do not look back…
Do not look back…
Girl:
Go on…
Why?
You are meant to fly.

<u>Didn't Know I Was Black</u>
A Memoir in Rhyme (Chapter 11)

Sacred Heart Academy date dance; circa 2003.

Didn't Know I Was Black
A Memoir in Rhyme (Chapter 11)

I didn't know I was black until I was 16.
These girls in the cafe sittin' in *with a lean.*
These white girls, my friends, started poking around
Asking all kinds of questions, *not trying to dumbfound.*

    "Where are you going to school in the fall?"

I poked out my chest and I stood… ***real tall.***

    "I'm going," I said, "…to an H.B.C.U."

What else…
Said, what else…
Said, what else would I do?

    "An H.C.U. *Um…*
    I'm sorry; *a what?"*

    "AN H.B.C.U."
I said from my gut.

She was talking out the side of her…
Talkin' out the side of her…
Talkin' out the side of her neck…

This girl she had me…
Girl she had me…
Girl she had me stressed.

And I didn't know.
Couldn't track.
Wasn't sure.

Couldn't sense.
Wasn't clear.
Didn't see why.

But, she was talking out the side of her neck...
Her neck...
And I was sitting there wondering why.

I was a senior at an all girls,
Predominantly white.
Yuh!
Private. Catholic School.
There were 6 black girls in my graduating class:
Each living a life of dual.
We were black girls, <u>sure.</u>
We were black girls...
Yet we were living in a world of white.
Our browns and blacks and caramels *weren't seen as marks of might.*

I loved my white friends, every one...
The Rachels, Brits and Blakes.
What wasn't to love?
My school was home.
I mean, for goodness sake...
I was a S.H.A. girl
Through and through.
Legit, from head to toe.
White shirts,
Gray skirts,
A sweater vest,
And knee highs down below...

Played volleyball.
Played basketball.
A student council rep.

I carried Sacred Heart inside with every single step.

Until that day, inside the cafe, when face to face to face…
I realized all the nuance of how I was claiming space.

>"Racism.
>That's racist!"

That's what this white child said.

>*"Racism:*
>An all black school."

It bounced 'round in my head…

Racism?
But how?
And why…
Why couldn't my friend see…?
In a school of browns and bronzes *I would get more free.*

>"Racism.
>It's just reversed.
>But, it's racist still.
>You can not have an all black school…
>Come on now, *be for real.*
>
>I'm sorry. I don't get it.
>It just doesn't make much sense…"

Deep breaths in.
Deep breaths out.
Do not take offense.

She was talking out the side of her…

Talkin' out the side of her…
Talkin' out the side of her neck…

This girl, she had me…
Girl she had me…
Girl she had me stressed.

And I didn't know.
Couldn't track.
Wasn't sure.
Couldn't sense.
Wasn't clear.
Didn't see why.

But, she was talking out the side of her neck…
Her neck…
While staring in my eyes.

"AN ALL WHITE SCHOOL!"

She powered on.

> "How would ***that*** make you feel?
> An all white school.
> ***An all white school.***
> Come on now, be for real.
>
> An all white school would bother you;
> It would not be fair…"

I looked around.
I shuffled.
Could I speak it?
Would I dare?

H-B-C-U
Mine came on through.
Showed me how to
Do what I do.
My H-B-C-
U, it taught me.
How to be free.
Centralize me.
Brown and Coffee
Chocolate. Toffee.
Mahogany, Tans,
Sepia, and
Every skin.
Yuh
All my kin.
Inside… Within
Had never been
Ignited, so
The flame did grow.
Hist'ry exposed.
And, grounded toes.
H-B-C-Us
Collated schools.
Teach brown kids that
They're genius, ***too.***
Do not teach hate.
Nor *separate.*
But that ***I'm*** great,
Can bare the weight,
Make the bent straight,
Ignore the bait.
Vict'ry's my fate.
'Spite of our state.
Others berate.
Will not abate.

Do not conflate.
Imma shoot straight.
Historically:
Black: *for me.*
Yuh!
College and University.
Historically:
Black: *for me.*
Yuh!
College and University.

She was talking out the side of her...
Talkin' out the side of her...
Talkin' out the side of her mouth...

She opened her head, her heart, *that day.*
And silly spilled right out.

And I didn't know.
Couldn't track.
Wasn't sure.
Couldn't sense.
Wasn't clear.
Didn't see why.

But, she was talking out the side of her neck...
Her neck...
While staring in my eyes.

I had no words that day.
...I know...
But step into my shoes...
I had so much, so much I say, I had so much to lose.

I did not even know that I was black until that day.

I did not even know, back then, but *oh -- **I know today.***

And today, as I look back; I look on with cheer.
I have a love, deep down inside, for my white friend-dear.
I only have a tiny thing I would like to say
If I could rewind, right now, to my blackening day:

"I live each day, friend, in a world that's almost wholly white.
This world has tried to force my hand and teach me white is right.
And, I am so excited about all that whiteness be.
But, also friend, I'm glad for blackness: bold and brave and free.

And I'm is black. That's what I am. That's all that I can be.
And I do pledge to love you, friend. You pledge to lovin' me?
A black school, friend, ain't racism. Like this school here, of white:
A black school, friend, empowers folks: blackness, *too*, is right."

My dear, sweet, friend… *Wherever she is…*
And should we meet again, I hope that she'll be proud of me ---
Stronger than back then…

Stronger now.
And smarter, too.
Mostly though, I hope;
Walkin' in my call from God
Snatchin' all my dope…

<u>Coming Undone</u>
An Extended Metaphor (Chapter 12)

A bike ride in Chandler, A.Z., a few months "before my button popped off";
August 2016.

Coming Undone
An Extended Metaphor (Chapter 12)

5 years ago…
In the land of A.Z.
My final button popped off and ran free:
My final button on my **best** shirt…
And it stumbled off chasing some dirt

In Arizona:
The gorge of the sun.
My button popped off.
I guess it was done:
Done with dust storms.
Done with the heat.
It rolled right past my feet.

In the middle of nothing:
A desert void.
The button popped off; I was **so** annoyed.
No. *No I wasn't.*
I was so scared.
Because suddenly <u>now</u> I was bare.

In a desert land,
I see it still,
I stood alone, (butt naked)
And wholly revealed.
I stood alone, (butt naked)
And petrified.
I figured *I might as well die.*

I had lost all my buttons ---
<u>Every</u> one…
And now I was standing, wholly undone.

I hadn't a button,
A zipper,
A hook.
And now I was standing there: shook.

I looked for a second,
A minute, then two...
I looked for a month...
And then for a few.
But I could not find it,
My button was gone.
"God, have I done something wrong?"

Why did it leave?
Where did it go?
Button gone: I had only a hole.
Button gone: there was growing space
Expanding and claiming its place.

The nights were long.
The days: ***too bright.***
And nothing, said nothing, said nothing fit right.
Of course nothing fit,
I hadn't a button
*And, it happened **-so-** all of the sudden.*

I talked to my monkey.
I talked to my mom.
I cried
Some days
Head into my palms.
But mostly I'd think through days too long:
Where has my button gone?

My therapist told me

I knew where it went.
She said,
"If you search, you will find a hint."
She was convinced
That it wasn't lost:
Advice... At an hourly cost.

My friends told me
"Girrrrrrl, I can't tell you when--
Was the last time I saw a bu-uh-tton."
That didn't help.
I didn't care.
I used to have buttons to spare.

I got so desperate one hot day.
I got so desperate,
So desperate I say.
I hollered a shout, so loud, so long ---
"Where has my button gone?"

I was paralyzed.
I couldn't progress.
Living less button was causing such stress.
Living less button was barely alive:
Hopelessness growing inside.

You have no clue of the worth of one stud.
But straight 'way I knew; I was hit with a thud.
It was suddenly clear. I could suddenly see.
My button was part of my free.

My shirt would not close.
My heart was exposed.
My heart was not strong.
My life was all wrong.

My heart was a mess.
My head was all stressed.
I wanted to hide all the problems inside.
But, my shirt would not shut.
I was left in a rut.
My chest was out: *free*
For the whole world to see.
But, my heart wasn't whole.
I had such ruth.
I was forced to face the truth.

Then one dark night inside of my room
When I was feeling so consumed
I looked around my hope-less space
And laid down on my face.

Cheek pressed,
Laid prostrate
Cheek to ground.
Though no one else could hear the sound...
Cheek pressed to ground
And heart in lay
And nothing else to say:

God.
God.
God.
God.
Something like a lightin' rod.
God.
Please.
God.
Help.
Barely whispers; couldn't yelp.
God.

Oh.
God.
Oh.
Still and quiet head to toe.
God.
I prayed:
All day…
All night…
Determined to get right.

God.
God.
God.
Please.

Help.
God.
Help me.

God.
God.
God.

I wutton [wasn't]…
Moving without my button.

I stayed
Face down
For year-long-days.
I stayed
Face down
I cried. I prayed.
I stayed
Face down
With eyes closed tight.

I had no strength to fight.

I stayed
Face down
For month-long-weeks.
I stayed
Face down
Floor meeting cheek.
I stayed
Face down
Then all of the sudden;
I looked… *and I saw…*

<u>MY BUTTON!!!</u>

.

.

.

.

.

.

.

.

.

.

.

I'm sorry.
Uh…
<u>What?</u>
Where have you been?
My button.
My lanta.
Could not comprehend.

Got to my knees.
Stood to my feet.

"Oh, my button!"
The meeting was sweet!

I never…
Not ever…
Not even today…
Found the appropriate words to say…

My button was lost
Then suddenly found.
But as I stopped to look around:
All had changed:
No desert land…
No raging storms of dust and sand.

I was suddenly planted, on fertile ground.
My button did not make a sound…
My button ran off
And made me chase.
Until I laid -*FLAT*- on my face.

I've found lots of buttons,
Since that day
Through peaceful nights of whispery prays.
Yes.
I am found.
Although I wutton.
Praise God for that button.

<u>Monkey</u>
A Short Poem (Chapter 13)

A hike with my monkey (Rob); circa 2020.

Monkey
A Short Poem (Chapter 13)

My monkey is the best;
He's loving me for me.
He doesn't care 'bout accolades.
He cares about my free.
He cares about my peace - my joy.
He cares about my mind.
I lost all my bananas, once.
He calmed me, "I'll share mine."

I Call My Hair Peaches (Part 1)
A Scene in Rhyme (Chapter 14)

Hair and body positive in full bloom a few weeks before the August 2019
Mrs. United States Pageant.

I Call My Hair Peaches (Part 1)
A Scene in Rhyme (Chapter 14)

Judge: I'm proud of you.

Me: Aw! *Thanks so much.*

Judge: I'm proud of you and all of your… ***stuff.***

Me: All of my… ***stuff?*** Wait… *Come again.*

Judge: I'm speaking to you as a friend.

     A pause.

Judge: You're beautiful.

Me: Thank you so much.

Judge: You're brilliant.

Me: Mm… *Not so much.*

Judge: And, girl, you made us all so proud.
     The whole entire crowd.

     A pause.

Me: I never thought that I would win.

Judge: I knew you would,
     You're brilliant, and--

Me: Well brilliant, sometimes, ain't the guide.
     Depend' on who decides…

A pause.

Judge: Your hair!
           Your platform --

Me: Thanking you

Judge: You're raw.
           And frank.
           You're bold.
           It's true.
           You're beautiful... *'spite what they say.*

Me: *Hm.*
           MmHm.
           Ok.

           A pause.

Judge: A pageant girl?

Me: Not usually.

Judge: Mm. Ok.
           I see. I see.

Me: Mhm.

Judge: Mhm.

Me: Mhm.

Judge: Ok.

A short breath:

Got one more thing to say.

A pause.

Judge: You could win at nationals.
            Win the crown for all **us... girls.**
            You could win.

Me: You think?

Judge: I do.
            Got one more thought for you.

       *Judge gives a long investigative look up and down taking in
            every inch of me.*

Me: Mm.

Judge: Mhm.

Me: Mhm.

Judge: Ok.

Me: Got.. one... more... thought... you'd... like... to... say?

Judge: Got one more thought.
            Mhm. I do.
            Got one more thought for you.

       A pause.

Judge: Your hair…

Me: Mhm.

Judge: Yes…

Me: Sisterlocks.

Judge: Your hair…
            It puts you in a box…

Me: A box?

Judge: Mhm.

Me: Ok?

Judge: Ok.
            Got one more thing to say.

            A pause.

Judge: Your weight.

Me: Mmhmm?

Judge: You're beautiful.

Me: Mm… Ok…

Judge: And, *this is bull.*
            But, pageants ain't for *gals like us:*
            Our weight… and hair… and ***stuff.***

            A pause.

Me: Mhm…

Judge: Mhm.
           But you could win.

Me: Mhm.

Judge: I'm talking as a friend.

Me: Mhm.

Judge: The world of pomp is strange.
           But…
           All you have to do is change.

I Call My Hair Peaches (Part 2)
A Poem (Chapter 15)

Moments after winning the Mrs. NJ United States Pageant; circa May 2019.
*An **actual** photo of the conversation from chapter 14...*

I Call My Hair Peaches (Part 2)
A Poem (Chapter 15)

I call my hair Peaches.
That ain't finna change.
I call my hair peaches,
I know it seems strange.
But peaches is fitting:
Sweet and strong...
As tough as the day is long.

I call my hair Peaches:
In all of her forms --
Locked or straightened she performs.
Shrunken coils and braided, too.
'Cause Peaches is my boo.

I call my hair Peaches.
Get with it, *k?*
I call my hair Peaches.
We ain't finna change.
If you don't like Peaches,
Then you don't like me.
It be... what it be... what it be...

It Is What It Is
An interlude (Chapter 16)

It be…
What it be…
What it be…
What it's been.
It is what it is…
You a friend?
You a friend…
You is or you ain't;
Ain't a problem for me…
Cause:
It be…
What it be…
What it be…

It is what it is…
And it ain't what it ain't.
It is what it is…
It cain't be what it cain't.
But I ain't fit'na change.
And, I'll say it again;
It is
What it be…
What it's been.

It is…
What it is…
What it is…
What it be.
Ain't no snatchin' my…
Snatchin' my…
Snatchin' my free…
It is what it is.

It's gone be what it be.
But know this:
You ain't takin' my free!

<u>Hair</u>
A Poem (Chapter 17)

Mrs. NJ photoshoot; circa Summer 2019.

Hair
A Poem (Chapter 17)

I'm black:
Bliggity black.
I'm bliggity black, black.

I'm black.
Right! Black.

Can you handle that?
Can you handle this?
Can you catch this throw?

I'm black.
I'm black.
I'm black: fa sho.

I'm black: that's right.
Yes:
Straight like that.

I'm black.
I'm black.
I'm bliggity black, black.

I'm black as I want to be:
Soul-deep black.

I'm black.
Bliggity black.
I'm bliggity black, black.

Don't like my fro.
Don't like my locs.

Don't like my kinks.
Like goldilocks?

Like straightened hair, *not kinks of crude?*
Like cheery blonde, **not black with 'tude?**

Don't like my crinks.
Don't like my curls.
Don't like my naps.
Don't like my swirls.

Don't like my brown.
That makes me blue.
But I won't stop;
My black is crew.

I'm black:
Bliggity black.
I'm bliggity black, black.
I'm black.
Right! Black.

Can you handle that?
Can you handle this?
Can you catch this throw?

I'm black.
I'm black.
I'm black: fa sho.
I'm black: that's right.
Yes:
Straight like that.

I'm black.
I'm black.

I'm bliggity black, black.

I'm black as I want to be:
Soul-deep black.

I'm black.
Bliggity black.
I'm bliggity black, black.

Don't like my cut.
Don't like my shave.
Don't like my fro.
Don't like my braids.
Don't like my perm.
Don't like my press.
Yo!
Hold up.
Wait.
<u>This has me stressed.</u>

Don't like my bald?
Don't like my bun?
Don't like my braids?
Not even one?
Don't like my hair?
Can't get no love?

From me to you: *a Kanye shrug!*

Because I'm black.
I'm black. You know?
Like deep inside – down in my soul:

Down – deep, deep, down – inside, I'm black.
It seems like you can't get with that.

And, I can't change this skin or hair.
I can't.
I won't.
I wouldn't dare.

I'm black.
That's right.
I'm bliggity black, black.

Don't like it?
Fine.
But, get with that.

Don't like my bangs.
Don't like my knots.
Don't like my weave that shines and POPS.
Don't like my glue.
Don't like my dye.
Don't like my fried, laid to the side.

Don't like my edges gelled and laid?
Don't like my wigs: one bold, one brave?
Don't like my slicked down Hollywood hair?
Don't like my mess-bun?
Think I care?

Don't like my fade.
Don't like my part.
Don't like my 'stache.
Don't think it's art?
Don't like my burns.
Don't like my beard.
Don't like my style.
You think it's weird.

But hey, you know what, here's the thing:
My me-ness makes my insides sing.
My me-ness touches every part:
My spirit, soul – my head and heart.

And you don't like my this or that.
'Cause all you see is bliggity black, black.
Yes, all you see is skin and hair.
<u>You haven't given soul a care.</u>

And yes: I'm black.
I'm bliggity black, black.
I'm black, black, black:
No hiding that.

I'm black: black skin.
I'm black: black hair.
I'm black: black styles.
And black: black cares.

But also deep inside I'm blue like skies and rains and oceans, too.
And also deep inside I'm white like clouds and smiles and God's bright light.

Deep down inside, I'm rainbow dyed.
I bet this comes as a surprise.
But here's the pie inside the sky:
There's always more than meets the eyes.

I'm black.
Bliggity black, ya'll.
Bliggity black, black.
I'm black, black, black:
No hiding that.

I'm black.

Bliggity black.
I'm bliggity black, black.
But I am much and that is fact.

Don't like my me.
I swear it's true.
Don't like my me 'less it's on you.
You like my hair atop your head.
You like my me on you instead.

But I like me from hair to heart.
Yes, I like me;
My black is art.
My black is every color made.
My black is free and strong and brave.

I'm black:
Bliggity black.
I'm bliggity black, black.

I'm black.
Right! Black.

Can you handle that?
Can you handle this?
Can you catch this throw?

I'm black.
I'm black.
I'm black: fa sho.

I'm black: that's right.
Yes:
Straight like that.

I'm black.
I'm black.
I'm bliggity black, black.
I'm black as I want to be:
Soul-deep black.
I'm black.
Bliggity black.
I'm bliggity black, black.

I saw this black girl;
Deep, dark black.
I saw this black girl,
Swear, it's fact.
I saw this black girl with this hair
That stretched and grew without a care.

Inside my dream this girl could fly.
Her kinks would take off towards the sky.
Her kinks would lift her to the clouds and then below a gathered crowd.

Beneath this girl I saw my kin:
My grandmama, a long lost friend.
My mama, grandpa, sweet thing, too.
Beneath this girl a great crowd grew.

Beneath this girl, beneath her hair, I saw the world with love and care.
I saw the moral, yes the point, that's meant to shine inside this joint:

Our skin, our hair, our features too
Connect us far beyond the blue,
Connect us way beyond the sky to ancestors who bled and died.
To ancestors who left this land hoping, praying, wishing and to ancestors who
knew back then:

<u>There's more than skin, there's heart – within.</u>

So you:
Be black.
Be bliggity black, black.

Be great and black.
Yes, straight light that.

Be black: black skin.
Be black: black cares.
Be black: black styles.
Be black: black hair.

But day by day. Be you.
Be you.

For be ye black or be ye blue.
Your you-ness is the key, you see.

So please be you.
And please, just be.

Turn Me Up
A Scene in Rhyme (Chapter 18)

Two of my all time favorite students (though there are too many to properly list)...
Phaedra Foreman (left), Osaivbie Igiebor (right);
circa 2021.

Turn Me Up
A Scene in Rhyme (Chapter 18)

Chaos pervades the space. Loud music. Arguing. Student 1 is out of control.
Yelling and pacing. No one listens to anyone; they can't even hear their own
voices.

Teacher: Who is you talking to?
               You ain't talkin' to me.

Student 1:   **What...** Teacher? I---

Teacher: What this, "**What** teacher..." be?
               Who this, "**What** teacher..." 'bout?
               'Cause child: <u>*you know better.*</u>

Student 2:   Teacher, he's under the weather.

Teacher: Yea? He better be.
               He done lost his mind--

Student 1:   No really... *I haven't.*
               I'm feeling just fine.

Student 2:   Ouuuuuuuuuuuuuuuu.

Student 3:   Wow.
Student 4:   Relax son. Chill.

Teacher: Oh... Oh ok.
               Nah, is that how you feel?

Student 1:   *This is my fault?*
               Be real.
               Come on.

Police men are trash.
How'm *I* in the wrong?

Student 3:   I don't e'en know.
*You **were** coming type crazy.*

Student 1:   This convo is making me hazy.

Teacher: That's real' convenient.
Perfectly timed.
Now you're feeling hazy…
Can't speak for your crime.

Student 2:   *(to Student 1)*
Fam… Just breathe…
For a second…
Or two…

Student 1:   Don't tell me what to do.

A beat.

Student 1:   I'm sorry.
Ok.
I just…
Don't understand.
It is what it is…
I'm is… *a man.*
I'm not a child.

Student 3:   Could've fooled me.

Teacher: You've got eyes child, but you
don't see.

Student 1:   What?

               A beat.
               Student 1 realizes that Teacher won't respond to, "What?" and then:

Student 1:   Teacher, *please ma'am.*
               I'm sorry;
               Explain.

Teacher: You got the answers, child: up in your brain.
               You tell me what happened.

Student 2:   You don't want to know...

Teacher: Tell me---

Student 3:   Unburden your soul...

               A beat.

               You **were** type wrong.

Student 4:   It is kinda true.

Student 1:   *Ugh!*
               She didn't...
               Ain't ask none of you!
               Ya'll type annoying. *Just --please-- shut up.*
               You all in my business stuff.

Teacher: Go on love.

Student 1:   Fine.
               But only for you.
               Ya'll can all leave...

Student 2:   What did I do?

Teacher: *(To Student 2)*
Baby, be quiet.
We're all wasting time.

Student 1:   Damn!
Sorry. Yes ma'am.
Ok.
Fine.

A beat. Student 1 continues:

I was headed to school,
Walking the block...

Student 4:   We were together,
You know how we rock.

Teacher: All of you babies?

Student 1:   Just us two…

Teacher glances at Student 4 to check in on the facts.

Student 4:   Yuh.
He's speaking it true.

Student 1:   *(To Teacher)*
You don't believe me?

Student 3:   You do like to lie.

Student 1:   What are you talkin' 'bout.
               And just… *Why?*
               Why are you here?

Teacher: *(To Student 3)*
               Sweetheart, please.
               Or I will have to ask you to leave.

Student 1:   Thank you.

Teacher: Go on.

Student 1:   Goodness.
               Damn.

Student 3:   Watch your mouth.

Student 1:   Sorry, ma'am.

Teacher: You're fine; go on.
               You were walkin' your street.

Student 4:   And this cop---

Student 1:   Was just posted, just lean't on his feet.

Student 4:   Fine.

Student 1:   We kept walking---

Student 4:   Making our way---

Student 1:   He was staring…like… *Damn,* **you got some'in to say?**

Student 4:   But we walked down the block.

Student 1:   As he stared with a gawk.

Teacher: Then…

Student 1:   We reached the end of the block.

Teacher: …*The end of the block*…

Student 4:   We was 'bout to turn---

Student 1:   Just tryin' to walk… my stomach churned…

Student 4:   About to turn---

Student 1:   But then suddenly son, my mans put his hand on his gun.

Teacher: What?

Student 1:   Ya dig?

Teacher: He pulled it out?

Student 4:   No.

Student 3:   A scream?

Student 2:   *A nag?*

Teacher: **A shout?**

Student 4:   Not from the cop…

Teacher: I'm sorry… *What?*

Student 1:   Be quiet. *Dang!!!* **Shut up.**

Student 4:   This fool got up---

Student 2:   *In the **cop's** face*...

Student 4:   *(pointing to Student 1)*
             He was wildin'---

Student 2:   Claimin' space...

Student 4:   This fool was yellin'... Spazzing out.

Teacher: What? I'm sorry.

Student 1:   *(to Student 4)*
             Shut your mouth!

Teacher: Watch *your* mouth
             Inside this place.
             This here is a sacred space.
             Have some 'spect,
             At least for me.
             Goodness.

Student 2:   *(to Student 1)*
             See!
             You see.

Teacher: Now.
             I'm confused.

Student 3:   No you ain't.

Teacher: Yes.
    I am.
    You couldn't--

Student 2: Can't…

Teacher: You can't be saying what I think…

Student 4: My heart was startin' to sink.

Teacher: You pressed him?

Student 3: Bro…

Student 2: …Could be dead.

Teacher: You pressed him?

Student 3: *What's in ya head?*

Teacher: **<u>You could be dead.</u>**

Student 1: I know.
    Oh well.
    That cop can go to hell.

Teacher: You… *Pressed him?*

Student 1: I'm sorry ma'am.
    But, really you gotta be mad at my mans.
    Hand on ya gun?
    Word? *Say less.*
    I live for a power flex.

Teacher (Internal Dialogue):

My kids have this jawn,
This song that they sang,
While they pop
And they clap
And they step
And they sway.

This song is so dumb
The silliest thing
But I can NOT stop hearing its
Nagging refrain.

Duhn. Duhn. Duhn. Duhn.
Turn me up.
Duhn. Duhn. Duhn. Duhn.
Turn me up.
Duhn. Duhn. Duhn. Duhn.
Turn me up.
Duhn. Duhn. Duhn. Duhn.
Turn me up.

Teacher: Wait.
            Come again.

Student 3: And, *louder this time.*

Student 2: You've lost your mind.

Student 4: He's lost his mind.

Teacher: You've lost your mind ---
            The whole darn jawn.

Student 1: I'd be proud if I was gone…

Teacher: You'd be proud?

Student 1:   Had I got murked...

Student 2:   What... I...

Student 3:   *What?*

Student 4:   You're bein' a jerk.

Student 1:   Nah. For real.

Student 2:   But why?

Student 3:   But... *why?*

Student 1:   I'm trying to live 'fore I die.

Teacher (Internal Dialogue):

My kids are so bright.
<u>My kids are so dumb.</u>
But when they're engrossed in all of their fun...
As I sit and stare...
I see traces of brilliance.
Each step boasts an epic resilience:

Duhn. Duhn. Duhn. Duhn.
Turn me up.
Duhn. Duhn. Duhn. Duhn.
Turn me up.
Duhn. Duhn. Duhn. Duhn.
Turn me up.
Duhn. Duhn. Duhn. Duhn.

Turn me up.

Student 1: I should **NOT** have to live on a street…
On a street…
Where a cop, with a smirk, all lean't on his feet
Can stare me down in the morn' as I walk
As I'm headed to school *on my block.*

I should **NOT** have to live in a world
In a world…
Where a cop shoots a woman, a man and a girl
Where a cop shoots to kill so perhaps he'll kill me,
If he lookin' and I'm what he see.

I'm **DETERMINED** to live 'fore I die.
I'm gone die…
But, I am not afraid and I'm telling you why:
I am not afraid because I will be free.
Nothing else *is* I'm willing to be.

Duhn. Duhn. Duhn. Duhn.
Turn me up.
Duhn. Duhn. Duhn. Duhn.
Turn me up.
Duhn. Duhn. Duhn. Duhn.
Turn me up.
Duhn. Duhn. Duhn. Duhn.
Turn me up.

Teacher: Respect little boy…

Student 3: Did you hear what she said?

Teacher: Respect little boy…

Student 3:   'Fore you ending up dead.

Teacher: Respect, said respect, yes for others.
              It's true.
              But mostly respect is 'bout you.
              What you lookin' like gone?
              What you lookin' like shot?
              What will that prove?

Student 3:   **Not a whole lot.**

Teacher: What will that prove?

Student 3:   Fool, she talkin' to you.

Teacher: *(to Student 3)*
              I'm talkin' to *you*, I say, too.

Student 1:   So I'm s'posed to just what ---
              Get over it...
              Take it?
              It's killin' me, Teacher.
              I'm s'posed to just fake it.

Teacher: It's killing you?

Student 1:   Right.

Teacher: And... You wantin' to thrive.
              And... **The goal is to keep you alive.**

              You think you don't matter;
              But really, you do.
              You think that ain't nobody checkin' for you.
              "Ya'll ain't checkin' for me,"; *Ha!* That's what you think.

And a boat filled with holes is destined to sink---

Student 4:   I'm checkin' for you.

Student 3:   Word. So are we.

Teacher: And *"we"* is how the hood get free.

Student 4:   And *we* ain't weak.

Student 3:   Nah! *We* gone fight.

Student 2:   But, *we* gone do it right.

Teacher: Turn me up. **Turn me up.**
Hear me real clear:
Your life is invaluable:
Precious --- *my dear.*

Turn me up louder. Pump-Pump me up.
There's waste around us --- all corrupt.
But, you can fight back. We got weapons at hand.
Our weapons ain't carved by the hands of man.
Our weapons are fierce - they can bring the house down.

Look:
They are all around.

Turn me up. **Turn me up.**
We should not be ignored.
At the top of each mountain, the furthest of shores...
Turn... I said turn... I said:
Put me on blast:
For the last shall be first and the first shall be last.
You may not feel counted, may not feel seen.

But I'm telling you baby, I say what I mean,
I know how you feel.
And here's what I'll say ---
This is the only way...

My weapon...
My weapon...
My weapon of choice...
Is my voice...
Is my voice...
Is my voice...
Is my voice...

I fight...
And I fight...
And I fight...
And I fight...
With my write...
With my write...
With my write...
With my write...

When it's looking real...
Looking real...
Looking real *bleak...*
I just open my mouth and I speak and I speak...

I feel evil surrounding from north to the south...
So I'll open my...
Open my...
Open my mouth...
You have so much power.
You don't even know.
You have so much power:
Your head to your toe.

You have so much power
And, so much to lose.

So,
What you gone...
What you gone choose?

Mr. Free and Ms. Run
A Poem (Chapter 19)

She stands on Central.
Claiming space.
Back bent.
Never straight.
Eyes rolling
Round her head…
Looking nearly dead.

He walks the streets:
Back and forth.
Steady.
Certain:
Stays the course.
Hair: luxurious,
Like a crown.
Never looking down.

She's lovely
Though I see her fade.
She dips and bops
Is she afraid?
I pray for her.
She's so far gone.
From dawn to dusk to dawn.

He's beautiful.
Embellished hair.
He walks the streets
Without a care.
He walks the streets.
But, is he well?
Really I can't tell.

She's in the street.
Eyes shut real tight.
She's in the street.
It isn't right.
I see her.
Hopin' she sees me:
Praying for her free.

Oblivious.
He is unphased.
Oblivious.
And looking dazed.
Oblivious.
But brilliant, still.
Present.
Raw.
And, real.

Quiet.
Frail.
Broken.
Brown.
Brilliance cloaked in mis'ry's gown.
We look *but do we really see:*
Ms. Run and Mr. Free?

Drugs?
Maybe.
Drugs…
Or life.
Or circumstance.
Or trauma rife.
But alas.
Here we be:
Aching to get free.

Mr. Free
With braided hair...
Living life without a care.
Mr. Free
I speak it true:
I'm praying just for you.

Ms. Run
Don't lose heart.
On that corner's
Just a start.
From that corner you will run
Right into the sun.

Mr. Free and Ms. Run
Your life has only just begun.
Don't believe a word they say:
Tomorrow ain't today.

And tomorrow,
You just may... be more free than you is today.
Hold your hope.
You ain't done.
You've only just begun.

Ms. Run and Mr. Free
Beautiful as they can be.
Beautiful **with all they stuff.**
They is part of us.

Ms. Run and Mr. Free
Beautiful as you can be.
Beautiful **with all your stuff.**
You are part of us.

<u>Skin</u>
A Poem (Chapter 20)

In my own skin; circa 2019.

Skin
A Poem (Chapter 20)

My *skin* is black.
Black skin ain't me.
I'm "a," and, "z."
1. 2. And 3.

"She this."
"He that."

You just *don't know.*
'Cause **skin** don't make
A girl or beau.

I'm black like night.
My skin is lush.
My skin is dark,
Like chalk – CO – LUT.
My skin can't crack.
It can't get old.
This brown – brown – baby, makes me **BOLD.**
This black – black – baby, makes me great.
It beams and glows and radiates.

But melanin;
It don't mean much;
It don't mean that I'm rough and tough.
It don't mean that I'm big and bad.
And some'a ya'll fools, you done been had.

Cause some'a ya'll fools, you got me bent.
You think that I'm irrelevant.
You think that I am dumb like bricks.
Because my skin is chalk – CO – LUT?
Naw, some'a ya'll fools gone get this straight

Yea, gather 'round, and don't be late.

My skin is black, fool.
Just my skin.
You know **not** what I am within.

My – **skin** – is black, fool.
Get it? Good.
'Cause **_skin_** don't make the brother, hood.

My **_skin_** is black.
It's just my skin.

Yea!
I got mother-land within.
Yea!
I got Malcom, Martin too.
And, I got pride.
And rep the crew.

But skin is skin.
And, skin ain't heart.
And, skin ain't soul or other parts.

Naw, skin is skin.
And skin ain't me.
Cause, "me," is more than eyes can see.

I'm white like snow.
I'm flawless white.
My skin is meek.
But, **meek with might.**
And, my skin changes:
White, then tan.
Sunburn comes, a peeling and –

I'm white again!
It's magical;
Mysteriously beautiful.
My skin is white.
But, guess what though —
I have a secret you don't know.

My skin is white
But *I am black.*
Black and proud.
Yea; "Black don't crack."
Yea; "Black like night."
Yes, me, jive fool.
Yo cuz'; I'm fam!
Yea! I'm black too!

I'm not like Rachel Dolezal.
I'm black, black, black;
My kin, and all.
My skin is white;
You hear me shout.
But yo fam. YO!
Don't count me out.
My skin is white.
But hey, *so what!*
I heard it said, "skin don't mean much."

Skin don't mean I don't struggle, too.
Skin don't mean I'm not down with you.
Skin white; so what? That ain't the whole?
What's the color of my soul?

My **skin** is black.
Black skin ain't me.
Yo! I am an anomaly.

My **<u>skin</u>** is black;
My skin, skin, skin.
But what about my hue within?

If you don't know me,
You can't say.
And skin ain't gonna give it 'way.
Naw skin ain't gonna give a clue.
Skin ain't jack; I tell it true.

And skin, skin, skin from east to west
Is black and white and brown and red.
There's blotchy skin with patches white.
There's tattooed skin with flyin' kites.
There's skin that scales and peels and bumps.
There's thick, scarred skin that came from cuts.
There's furry skin, like cats and dogs.
And slimy skin on toads and frogs.
There's skin with rings.
There's skin with spots.
There's even skin with spots a lots.
There's skin that wrinkles, hangs and sags.
There's skin, near eyes, that look like bags.
There's skin;
There's ne'er a drought of skin.
But what about the soul within?

My **<u>skin</u>** is black.
<u>Black skin ain't me.</u>
I'm "a," and, "z."
1. 2. And 3.

"She this."
"He that."

You just *don't know.*
'Cause **skin** don't make
A girl or beau.

My **skin** is black.
It's just my skin.

Yea!
I got mother-land within.
Yea!
I got Malcom, Martin too.
And, I got pride.
And rep the crew.

But skin is skin.
And, skin ain't heart.
And, skin ain't soul or other parts.

Naw, skin is skin.
And skin ain't me.
Cause, "me," is more than eyes can see.

My **skin** is black.
Black skin ain't me.
Yo! I am an anomaly.
My **skin** is black;
My skin, skin, skin.
But what about my hue within?

If you don't know me,
You can't say.
And skin ain't gonna give it 'way.
Naw skin ain't gonna give a clue.
Skin ain't jack; I tell it true.

I tell it, tell it. Tell it 'gain.
I scream it, scream it, scream it and ---
I'm hoping, hoping, hoping – friend.
I'm praying you'll look past my skin.

I'm praying, praying, praying loud.
I'm screaming it to every crowd,
I'm lifting up my voice real high.
I'm lifting it into the sky.

I'm proud. You know.
I'm proud. It's true.
I'm proud 'bout me.
I'm proud 'bout you.
I'm beautiful.
I love my skin.
But more, I love the me within.

And more, I wish.
I tell it true;
I wish one day that me and you could meet.
I wish.
I wish, dear friend;
That we could meet.
No!
Not our skin.
I wish one day that we could meet.
A soul to soul style hug and greet.

Look up. Look up.
Look to the sky.
You see. You see.
Both you and I.
We were created:
Soul and heart.

Yes.
Those are the important parts.
And, that's what makes a human whole.
Not skin.
Not hair.
It's heart and soul.
It's heart and soul.
Dear friend.
Dear friend.
It's not a matter of the skin.

I pray, pray, pray.
I tell it true.
I hope, hope, hope,
For me and you.
I hope and pray,
One day, my friend.
That you will see:
my black....
Is skin.

<u>Broadway</u>
A Poem (Chapter 21)

My Associate Directorial Debut on Broadway with the musical Company;
a day of rehearsal at the theater. November 2021.

The neon lights *are* bright,
On 45th and 8th.
The stage door stands: a beacon of glory
In every alleyway.
But here's one thing I'm finding now
I only partially knew:
The only thing that's missing here is…
Me…
And you…
And you.

That Ain't the Standard
A Poem (Chapter 22)

Pictures from the "I Can Be," Mrs. NJ campaign, Circa 2019.
These are women who set the standard, everyday.

That Ain't the Standard
A Poem (Chapter 22)

That ain't the standard;

You is.
You is.

That ain't the standard;
And, *this ain't a quiz.*

You're framing this test.
They checkin' on you?
Uh…
No.
Uh… *sorry…*
They checkin' on who?

"They" ain't the standard.
The standard is you.
You is the standard.
You are… *It's true.*

You are the standard
Get that in ya' head.
Etch it inside with a pen that is red.

You are the standard.
You is.
You are!

You are the mark.
You are the gold star.

Stop shooting for something so far and away…

You have it.
You've got it.
You own it.
Ok?

You ain't gotta change.
Said; Don't. Change. ****.
You ain't gotta change.
That's all.
That's it.
Don't change.
<u>Don't change.</u>
You is enough.
Don't change,
Not one thing...
None of your stuff.

What you gone change?
And why?
For what?
Ain't no ifs or ands or buts…
You the standard.
You is.
You.
Don't you change for nothin' boo.

You is great.
And, you is good.
You is enough.
In *every* hood.
And if someone ain't with it, well ---
That "someone" can go straight to hell.

We always looking out,
Yes out…

We always looking in… with doubt.
But out we looking ---
Way out there,
For what to be and who and where
And why and how…
We looking out.
We always looking in… with doubt.
But then we looking way outside
For, *WHAT,* some kind of guide?

But, that ain't it.
It isn't out;
Even with the inward doubt.
Even with the doubt inside,
The outside can not be your guide.

It ain't the standard.
That ain't it.
That,
Or they,
Or theirs,
Or them…
That…
That…
That…
Ain't it.
Ain't it.

Bet on *you.*
Don't quit.

Acceptance Speech
A Poem (Chapter 23)

Getting ready for a performance of "12 Mo' Angry Men" @ LaTea Theatre, NYC, closing night; circa October 2021.

Acceptance Speech
A Short Poem (Chapter 23)

I've been rehearsing my speech.
So, I know what I'll say.
I've been rehearsing my speech for my great *gettin' up day.*
And no matter the stage, and no matter the time, I've been rehearsing my speech --
- and the speech is all mine;

THE EGOT (Reprised)
A Speech (Chapter 24)

Stop waiting to be counted.

Ha!

You waitin' to just... Be?
Stop waiting to get free.
It be what it be.

Here you are: *here ---*
Go on!!!
Snatch back yo' free.
You ain't got nothin' else, think we all can agree:

You're just wasting your time sittin' 'round to be tapped.

Waitin' for this.
Then **you** waitin' for that.
*What **you** waitin' for, bruh?*
The time is now.
'Nother second of waiting, can not be allowed...

Ain't nobody gone choose you.
You ain't gone be tapped.

Our world simply isn't....

It ain't set up for that.

No matter your call...
No matter your fight...
Someone always gon' say,
"You ain't doin' it right."

The world ain't for rebels.
What... **_you got a cause?_**
I hope you ain't waitin' or 'spectin' applause.
The world is set up for herding the sheeple.
YOU ain't no sheeple though...***people.***

So much is wasting:
Time...
Thought...
And the waitin'... **the waitin' is mostly for naught.**

Here is the secret...
Here is the key:

You ain't waitin' on nothin';
You're free!

You don't need no approval... **You don't need it, friend.**
You don't need no one else; you can simply begin.

The praise and the blame...
They just 'bout the same
But, the name of the game
Is stop chasing the fame.

Stop chasing the fame,

That's the name of the game.
'Cause the blame got you crazed
And the praise is to blame.

It ain't about fame.
If you're blamed,
If you're praised
Keep this in frame:
Play **_your_** best game.

So this one right here ---
This goes out to the homies;
The world may not give you a treasure or trophy.
The world may not get---
You're ahead of your time...
And, too far ahead is treated as crime.
But, way out ahead is paving the way.
And, way out ahead, despite what they say;
Is what change the world.

That is a fact.

And it ain't...
Ain't no rhyme beat for that.

God's got you inside out, *ya hear?*
He's got you all around.
You haven't even got to call ---
Least of all aloud.

God, I said...
God's got you.
He's got you where you lack.
Back
To front

To back
To front
To front
To back
To back.

So;
Go.
Go back.
Go take yo' stuff.
Yo' stuff.
Go back.
Go' get yo' stuff.

That **stuff?**
That stuff…

It ain't just stuff.

That, "stuff"…
Is yours,
It ain't enough:
A sorry?

No!

No; that won't do.

That stuff…
That stuff
Belong to you.

Go.
I say.
Where'er it be.

Go back and get yo' free.

And;
Stay.
Face down
For year-long-days.
Said stay --
Face down
And cry. *Or pray.*
Yes stay --
Face down
With eyes closed tight.

I know sometimes it's hard to fight.

But stay,
Face down
For month-long-weeks.
And stay,
Face down
Floor meeting cheek.
Yes stay
Face down
'Til suddenly...
You snatchin' back yo' free.

Free!
Yes, free.
Yes.
Free.
Free!
Free.
Chained at first *then suddenly...*
Chained at first and whipped and down...
But suddenly with head to ground...

Yes!
Free.
Free.
Free!
<u>Free.</u>
<small>Free.</small>
Free.

Free.

Free of E-G-O-*and T.*
Free to be whate'er you be.
Free to fly.
Yes!
Boundlessly.
It is what it is…
What it is…
What it be…

You is lookin' real…
Lookin' real:
Free.

<u>*Who?*</u>

I said:
<u>*Who?*</u>

I said:
<u>*Who?*</u>

I said:
<u>*Who?*</u>

<u>The worth of your life is determined by you!</u>

The worth of your life ain't determined by me.

<u>So,</u>
Go snatch all your *E.G.O.Ts*.

Photo Book

Through the Years...

(Left) Tea & Mom (Pamela Fordham); Circa 1988. (Right) Grandma (Freddie Mae Fordham) & Tea; Circa 1990.

Tea and Gabe James at the Sacred Heart Academy date dance; Circa 2003.

(Left) Newark Collegiate Academy students; circa 2018.
(Right) NCA students and Mrs. Tea (center with hat); circa 2018.

(Left) Tea & student (Jaden Charles) at George Floyd Monument, Newark, NJ; circa 2021.
(Right) Tea & student (Osaivbie Igierbor) hiking in NJ; circa 2020.

Tea & Rob, Tea's favorite guy in the world; circa 2021.

The "Queens Do..." Mrs. NJ campaign by TaNisha Fordham; circa 2019.
Campaign continues below:

(From top left) "Queens remember." "Queens don't take themselves too seriously." "Queens keep first things first." "Queens pray." "Queens eat chips." The "Queens Do…" campaign was inspired to encourage people to be comfortable in their own skin; circa 2019.

Mrs. NJ speaking engagement Queens, NY; circa 2019.

TaNisha Fordham; Summer 2021

TaNisha Fordham
THE EGOT

<u>Reflections</u>

*Now it's your turn; Now that you've read my story... What will **<u>you</u>** do? Write it down. What is your heart speaking to **<u>you</u>** right now?*

Visit our site and share how this book has inspired you:
www.enlightenedvisions.org

"It's in your bones; *ignore the chatter*.
<u>Only **your** thoughts matter.</u>
It is your call; *your destiny*.
Go'on --- **snatch yo' free.**"

#tanishafordhamtheegot
#snatchyofree

<u>Save your reviews.</u>
Go on...
Put 'em away.
Save your reviews
'Less you' givin' an A.

'Less you' givin' an A
And I'm talking... *to start...*
<u>Ain't no reviewing the stuff from my heart.</u>

Ain't no review.
I mean...
<u>Where d'ey do that?</u>
You scoring my heart?!?
Ain't no tallying that.

Ain't no tallying passion...
No scoring my free.
Nah bruh.
You ain't tallying...
Me.

I said what I said.
I said:
Save your reviews.
I said what I meant
And I'm speaking it true.

This... This right here is my heart's pitter pat.
And how you be tallying that?

<u>I showed up today.</u>
I showed up as me.
You didn't like it?
Well:
Here I'm is...
FREE.
So, it is what it is
And, it be what it be.
Ain't no tallying something that's free.

Thank you God.
Amen.